NATIONAL ART EDUCATION ASSOCIATION

Design Standards
for School Art Facilities

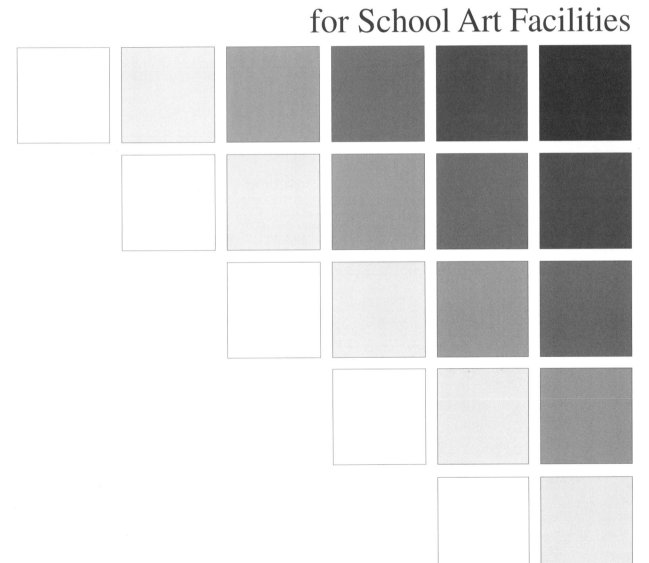

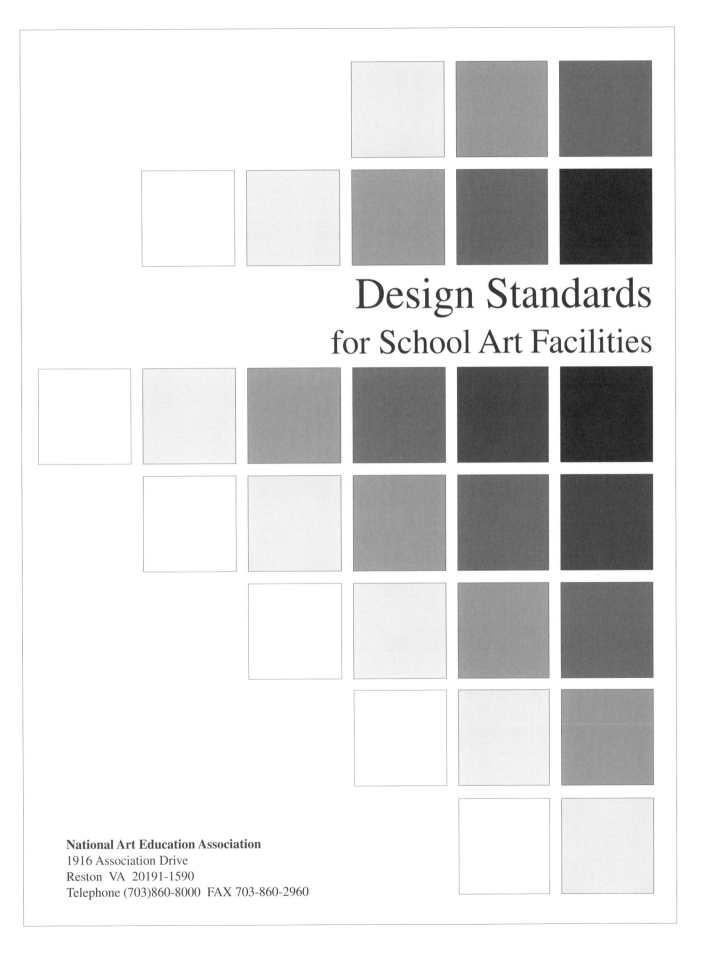

Design Standards
for School Art Facilities

National Art Education Association
1916 Association Drive
Reston VA 20191-1590
Telephone (703)860-8000 FAX 703-860-2960

About NAEA …

Founded in 1947, the National Art Education Association is the largest professional art education association in the world. Membership includes elementary and secondary teachers, art administrators, museum educators, arts council staff, and university professors from throughout the United States and 66 foreign countries. NAEA's mission is to advance art education through professional development, service, advancement of knowledge, and leadership.

© 1994, National Art Education Association, 1916 Association Drive, Reston, VA 20191-1590.

ISBN 0-937652-65-2

PREFACE

It is difficult to address in depth all of the intricacies of facilities planning in one publication. Synthesizing programmatic requirements, preferences, and local building codes made the development of this publication a formidable task. The purpose of this guide is to serve as a general planning reference. It was impossible to replicate all the codes, the requirements, the legislation, even the educational program requirements for the nation's nearly 16,000 school districts. While the committee focused their attention on the design and educational requirements for planning art facilities, we do not wish to diminish the importance of current attention on safety in the art room, hazards in using art equipment and materials, as well as providing a barrier free environment for students. We have provided a listing of sources, agencies, manufacturers, organizations, and state and Federal offices that should be utilized for current data and information.

The National Art Education Association (NAEA) began work on this initiative in 1989. The initial draft was based on a survey of over ninety different constituencies, including school districts and state education agencies. The NAEA appointed a national committee to develop and refine the first draft. Upon completion of the second draft, the committee sought input through the *NAEA News*. The second draft was then sent to state art association presidents, Delegates Assembly, affiliates, state directors of art education, state newsletter editors, and SHIP members. The final publication represents the views of this broad-based constituency, as well as the architectural and school planning communities.

The *Design Standards for School Art Facilities* committee developed the most comprehensive document possible given the diverse target audiences. The committee structured this document around the grade level organizational patterns commonly used by schools and districts.

I am most appreciative of Thomas A. Hatfield and the staff at the NAEA office for their assistance in taking this publication to press. My final thanks go to the members of the NAEA *Design Standards for School Art Facilities* committee and to the members who provided the photographs used as visual illustrations throughout the document. They provided valuable insight during the development of this document in assuring that NAEA's integrity was reflected.

I trust that facility planners will find this publication useful in creating art education environments for our young citizenry.

Mac Arthur Goodwin, *Committee Chair and Editor*

Committee Members

Ray Azcuy, Florida; Sam Banks, Virginia; Vicki Bodenhamer, Mississippi; Isabelle Bush, Georgia; Woody Duncan, Kansas; Thomas L. Garguillo, North Carolina; Michael T. Gilliatt, Virginia; Adriennne Hoard, Missouri; Norbert Irvine, North Carolina; Nicholas Kyle, Oklahoma; Trini Lopez, Texas; Pam McGill, South Carolina; Carol Pugh, Virginia; Charles A. Qualley, Colorado; Alan Sandler, District of Columbia; Sarah Tambucci, Pennsylvania; Patty Taylor, California; Taft Utermohle, Maryland; Barbara Weinstein, Pennsylvania; Nan Yoshida, California; Bernard Young, Arizona; *Ex-Officio Members:* James Clarke, NAEA President; Thomas A. Hatfield, NAEA Executive Director; Beth McDavid, Elementary Division Director; Martin Rayala, Supervision/Administration Division Director.

TABLE OF CONTENTS

PLANNING AN ART ROOM: INTRODUCTION

Facilities needs and requirements for creative art activities are as varied as the individual differences between schools, teachers, and curricula. To broaden the areas of instruction and learning, rooms and equipment must be more specialized to meet the needs of a diversified program.

The success of an art program depends to a considerable degree on how much thoughtful planning and consideration is given to the facility and how much money is made available for it. Yet the ultimate responsibilities for these issues are rarely in the hands of the art educator. It is therefore imperative for the school administrator to involve the art teacher in decisions concerning the budget for the room, materials and equipment, and similar matters.

Below: Panoramic view art room. Ralph M. Captain School, Clayton, MO.

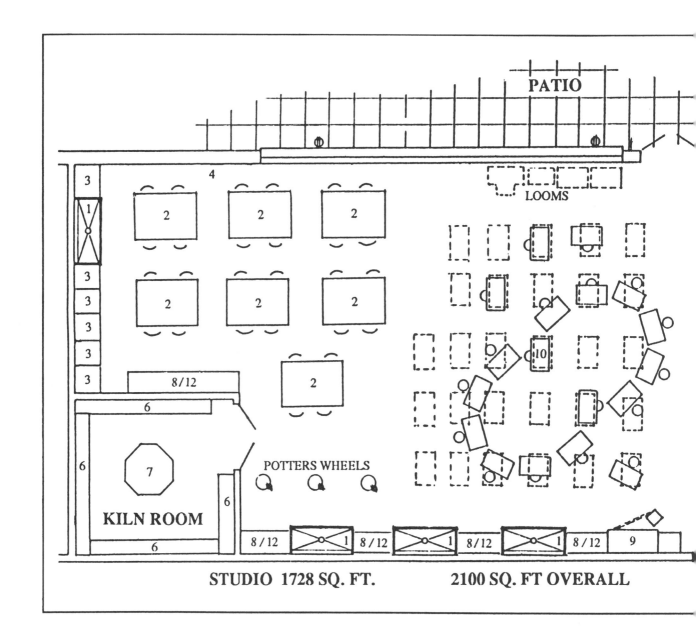

PATIO

LOOMS

3
1
3
3
3
3
3

4

2   2   2

2   2   2

8/12

2

6

6

7

KILN ROOM

6

6   POTTERS WHEELS

10

8/12   1   8/12   1   8/12   1   8/12   9

STUDIO 1728 SQ. FT.   2100 SQ. FT OVERALL

Many activities—besides the easily thought of drawing and painting in various media—will be carried on in the art room. Therefore, a well-planned art facility needs electronic access and proper storage to provide for (1) graphic arts, including computer graphics, block printing, etching, and lithography; (2) general crafts such as metals and weaving; (3) modeling; (4) sculpting; and (5) ceramics. The space must also be flexible enough to facilitate student discussions, viewing slides, and reproductions.

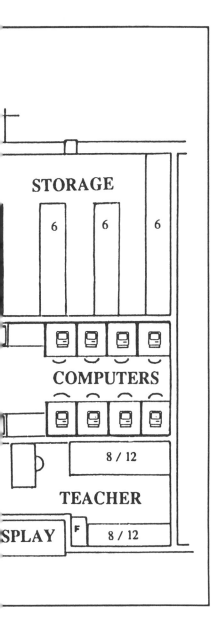

STORAGE

6   6   6

COMPUTERS

8 / 12

TEACHER

SPLAY   F   8 / 12

Left: All Purpose Art Studio — Modification from *Educationally Correct Art Studios,* Sheldon/ General Equipment Manufacturers, Crystal Springs, MS.

Code:

1. Sink with sedimentary trap.
2. Student tables.
3. Floor-to-ceiling cabinet.
4. Chalkboard.
5. Bulletin Board.
6. Shelving.
7. Kiln/Ventilation system.
8. Counter.
9. Screen/Projection center.
10. Drawing stations.
11. Paper storage.
12. Overhead storage.
13. Press.
14. Drying rack.
15. Light table.

For such a variety of experiences, adequate space, including storage space, and a range of equipment and supplies should be provided. Work centers and equipment should be carefully planned with appropriate traffic lines between them. In planning the art room, special provision should be made for mobility and flexibility in the use of equipment in the room, and for making a variety of materials available quickly and systematically. It is also imperative that adequate display and storage areas be provided in the art room for two- and three-dimensional projects.

The room should be designed to accommodate no more than 28 students at the elementary level, 24 students at the junior/middle level, and accommodate 20 students at the senior level. Differences in the curriculum cause the varying numbers of each level. Similarly, the number of art rooms per building varies depending on the number of students enrolled in school. A reliable gauge is one art room per 500 students enrolled in the school. For example, a school with 1,500 enrollment should have three art rooms, a school of 2,000 four art rooms, and so forth. One similarity, however, is the amount of storage space needed per student: regardless of grade level, each student in a successful art program should be provided with 55 square feet of net floor space, exclusive of storage space, a kiln room, a computer, multimedia laboratory, and teacher's office.

Special attention should be given to the overall design of the junior/middle and senior high art rooms. Because the program of study includes a broad diversity of art media and academic experiences, it is desirable that art rooms have a studio-like atmosphere and an appearance quite different from the ordinary classroom.

If at all possible, locate the art room on the school's first floor. This simplifies both displaying student art (which is visual education

General view of art rooms. *Top left:* New Horizons Elementary School, West Palm Beach, Florida.
Top right: Sarah W. Starkweather Elementary School, West Chester Area School District, West Chester, PA.
Opposite top: Hattiesburg High School, Hattiesburg, MS.
Opposite middle: D.H. Conley High School, Pitt County Schools, Greenville, NC.
Opposite bottom: Winter Haven High School, Winter Haven, FL.

for the whole school) plus the delivery of materials and supplies to the department as well as encouraging the outdoor activities of sketching, painting, modeling, and construction.

It is also desirable to locate the art room as close as possible to other visual and performing arts areas so that activities between these areas can be coordinated.

General lighting should be planned so that shadows are reduced to a minimum in all parts of the room. Lighting the color of daylight will permit accuracy of color work, regardless of the changing outdoor conditions. Computer graphics and multimedia equipment should be in a separate room.

Other furnishings should be arranged for maximum flexibility, keeping in mind, however, that a teacher rarely has the time to rearrange furniture between the dismissal of one class and beginning of the next. The sinks — very important items in any art room — should be accessible from more than one side. One sink can accommodate ten students adequately. Sinks should be equipped with

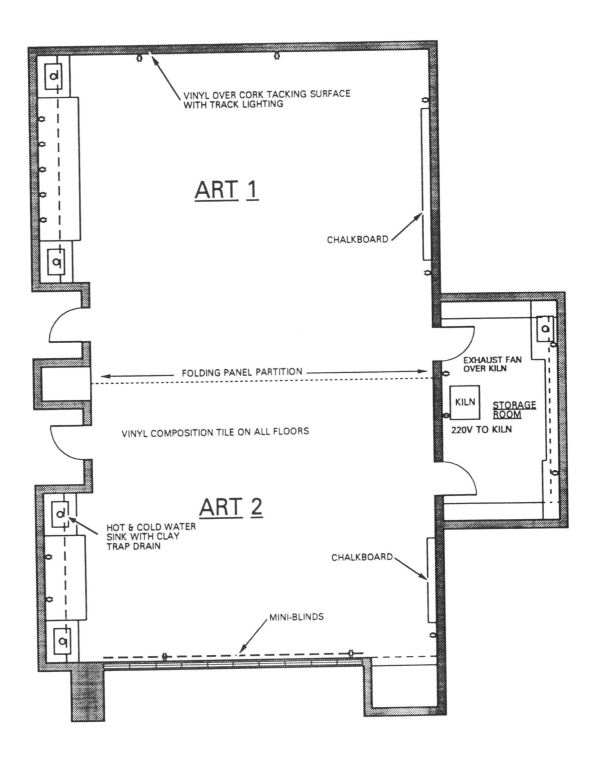

ART 1

VINYL OVER CORK TACKING SURFACE
WITH TRACK LIGHTING

CHALKBOARD

FOLDING PANEL PARTITION

EXHAUST FAN
OVER KILN

KILN

STORAGE
ROOM

220V TO KILN

VINYL COMPOSITION TILE ON ALL FLOORS

ART 2

HOT & COLD WATER
SINK WITH CLAY
TRAP DRAIN

CHALKBOARD

MINI-BLINDS

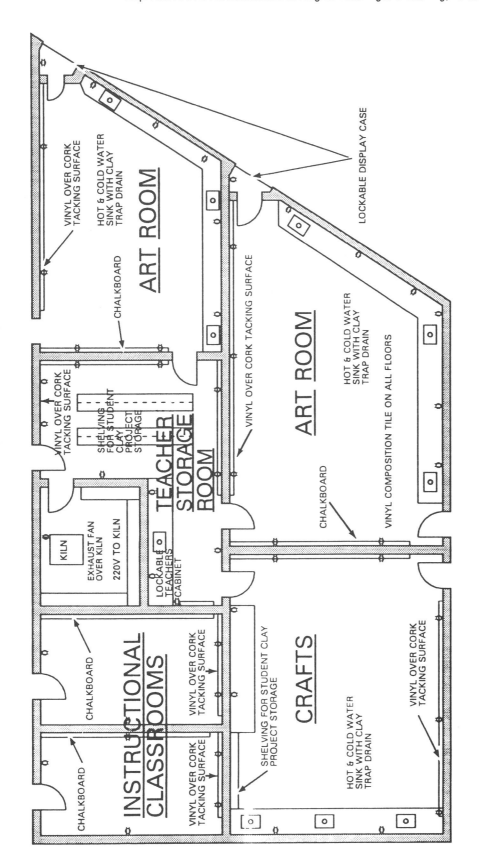

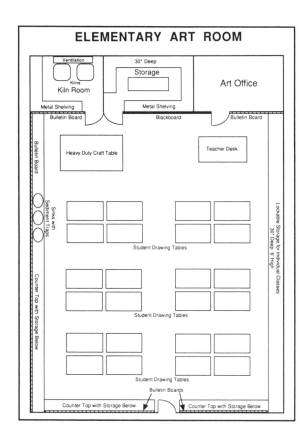

ELEMENTARY ART ROOM

(Floor plan labels, clockwise from top:) Ventilation; 30" Deep Storage; Art Office; Kilns; Kiln Room; Metal Shelving; Metal Shelving; Bulletin Board; Blackboard; Bulletin Board; Heavy Duty Craft Table; Teacher Desk; Bulletin Board; Sinks with Sediment Traps; Student Drawing Tables; Lockable Storage for Individual Classes 30" Deep; 6' High; Counter Top with Storage Below; Student Drawing Tables; Student Drawing Tables; Bulletin Boards; Counter Top with Storage Below; Counter Top with Storage Below

hot and cold water with sediment traps. Kilns should be located in a separate room with appropriate ventilation.

Elementary Schools

There should be one art room with one art teacher for every 400-500 students. The art room should have at least 55 square feet of work space per student (excluding storage and teacher's work space) and be flexible enough for use with large or small groups and for individual instructional activities.

Cover at least one wall with cork-board from floor to ceiling for displaying student work. Display areas such as shelves and cases should also be provided for three-dimensional work like sculpture and ceramics. These areas should be well lighted and equipped with multiple lighting plug-in tracks with movable spotlights.

Adequate in-class storage, accessible to students, is needed as well as at least 350 square feet of lockable storage space for art supplies, equipment and student art works. This latter space should be connected to the art room (see Storage).

Middle/Junior High Schools

There should be one art room with one art teacher for every 400-500 students. The art room should have at least 55 square feet of work space per student (excluding storage and teacher's work space) and be flexible enough for both group or individual instructional activities. Adequate design should allow for ease of traffic flow and adequate space should be planned for special furniture and equipment. A wet area with a sink is desirable for clay work. If facility planning includes a patio, it should be located near the art room.

Cover at least one wall with cork-board from

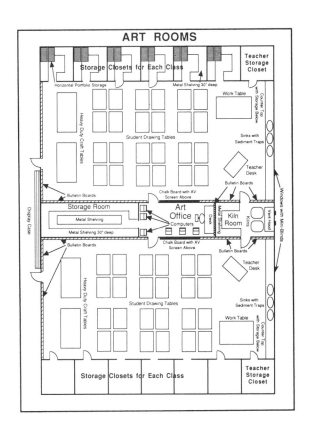

ART ROOMS

Opposite page: Sample all purpose elementary art room with teacher office, lockable storage, and vented kiln room.
This page top: Dual multipurpose art rooms with shared teacher office, kiln room, and storage room. Note specialized class storage closets for student works-in-progress.
Middle right: Winter Haven High School, Winter Haven, Florida.
Bottom right: Children's Art Resource Center, Virginia Museum of Fine Arts, Richmond, Virginia. Note that worktables tilt from wall and the adjacent storage units.

Middle School, Arlington Independent School District, Arlington, TX.
Reproduced from *Art Education: Planning for Teaching and Learning*, Texas Education Agency

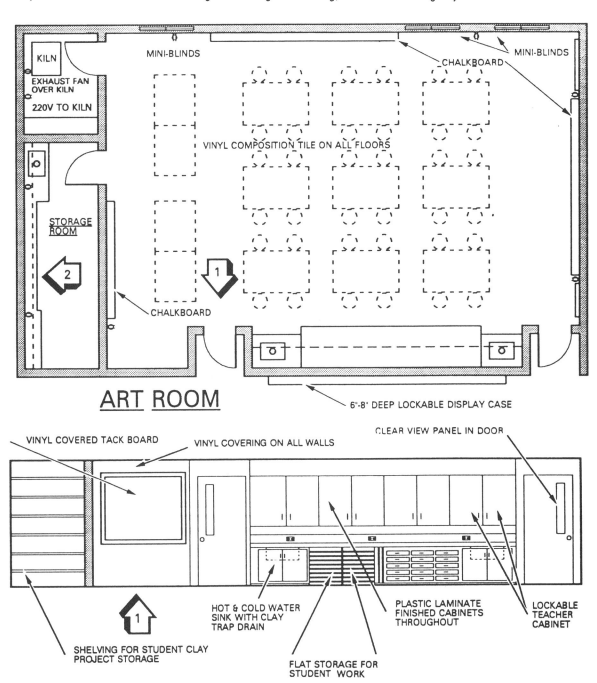

ART ROOM

KILN
EXHAUST FAN OVER KILN
220V TO KILN
STORAGE ROOM
2
MINI-BLINDS
CHALKBOARD
MINI-BLINDS
VINYL COMPOSITION TILE ON ALL FLOORS
1
CHALKBOARD
6"-8" DEEP LOCKABLE DISPLAY CASE

VINYL COVERED TACK BOARD
VINYL COVERING ON ALL WALLS
CLEAR VIEW PANEL IN DOOR
1
HOT & COLD WATER SINK WITH CLAY TRAP DRAIN
PLASTIC LAMINATE FINISHED CABINETS THROUGHOUT
LOCKABLE TEACHER CABINET
SHELVING FOR STUDENT CLAY PROJECT STORAGE
FLAT STORAGE FOR STUDENT WORK

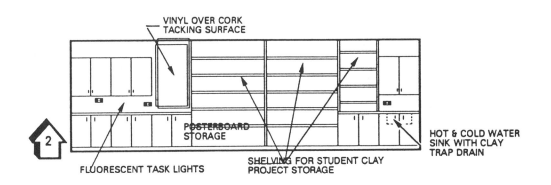

VINYL OVER CORK TACKING SURFACE
2
POSTERBOARD STORAGE
HOT & COLD WATER SINK WITH CLAY TRAP DRAIN
FLUORESCENT TASK LIGHTS
SHELVING FOR STUDENT CLAY PROJECT STORAGE

10

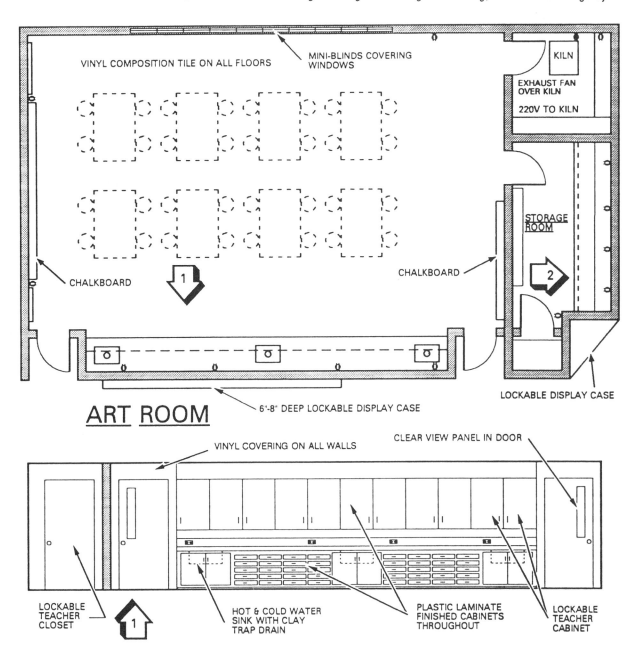

VINYL COMPOSITION TILE ON ALL FLOORS

MINI-BLINDS COVERING WINDOWS

KILN

EXHAUST FAN OVER KILN

220V TO KILN

STORAGE ROOM

CHALKBOARD

CHALKBOARD

1

2

6"-8" DEEP LOCKABLE DISPLAY CASE

LOCKABLE DISPLAY CASE

ART ROOM

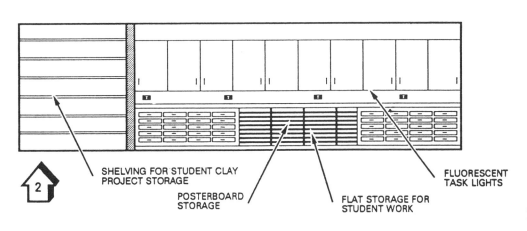

VINYL COVERING ON ALL WALLS

CLEAR VIEW PANEL IN DOOR

LOCKABLE TEACHER CLOSET

1

HOT & COLD WATER SINK WITH CLAY TRAP DRAIN

PLASTIC LAMINATE FINISHED CABINETS THROUGHOUT

LOCKABLE TEACHER CABINET

2

SHELVING FOR STUDENT CLAY PROJECT STORAGE

POSTERBOARD STORAGE

FLAT STORAGE FOR STUDENT WORK

FLUORESCENT TASK LIGHTS

floor to ceiling for displaying student work and visual aids. Display areas such as shelves and cases should also be provided for three-dimensional work like sculpture, ceramics, and jewelry. These areas should be well lighted and equipped with multiple lighting plug-in tracks with movable spotlights.

Adequate in-class storage, easily accessible to students, is needed as well as at least 400 square feet of lockable storage space for art supplies, equipment and student art works. This latter space should be connected to the art room (see Storage).

Secondary Schools

There should be one art room with one art teacher for every 500-600 students. The art room should have a minimum of 55 square feet per student, excluding storage and teacher's work space and be flexible enough for use with group or individual instructional activities. Adequate design should allow for ease of traffic flow and adequate space should also be planned for special furniture and equipment such as easels, potter's wheels, floor looms, and darkroom developing tanks and enlargers. A wet area with a sink is desirable for clay work. If a patio is provided, the wet area should be located near it.

In addition to in-class storage, at least 400 square feet of lockable storage space should be provided for art supplies, equipment and student art works and to prevent student access to potentially dangerous equipment or materials. This storage space should be connected to the art room (see Storage).

At least one wall should be designed for displaying student work and visual aids, i.e. fine art reproductions, i.e. cork-board from floor to ceiling. Display areas should be provided for three-dimensional work, i.e., shelves and cases for sculpture, ceramics, and jewelry. These areas should be well lighted and equipped with multiple lighting plug-in tracks with movable spotlights.

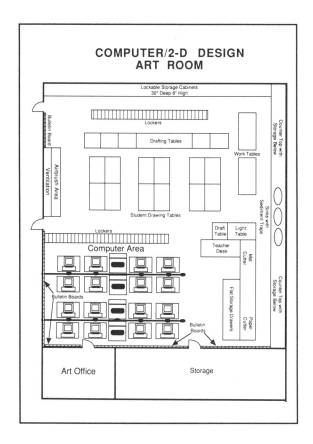

COMPUTER/2-D DESIGN ART ROOM

Lockable Storage Cabinets 30" Deep 6" High

Lockers

Drafting Tables

Work Tables

Student Drawing Tables

Bulletin Board

Airbrush Area

Ventilation

Counter Top with Storage Below

Sinks with Sediment Traps

Lockers

Computer Area

Bulletin Boards

Draft Table

Light Table

Teacher Desk

Mat Cutter

Paper Cutter

Flat Storage Drawers

Counter Top with Storage Below

Bulletin Boards

Art Office

Storage

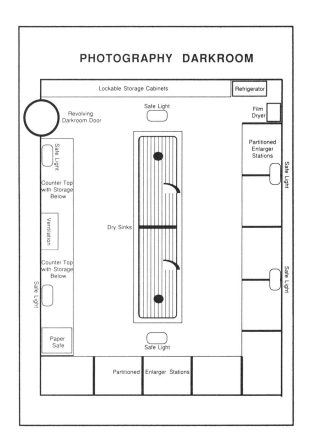

PHOTOGRAPHY DARKROOM

Lockable Storage Cabinets

Refrigerator

Revolving Darkroom Door

Safe Light

Film Dryer

Safe Light

Counter Top with Storage Below

Ventilation

Counter Top with Storage Below

Safe Light

Paper Safe

Dry Sinks

Partitioned Enlarger Stations

Safe Light

Safe Light

Safe Light

Partitioned Enlarger Stations

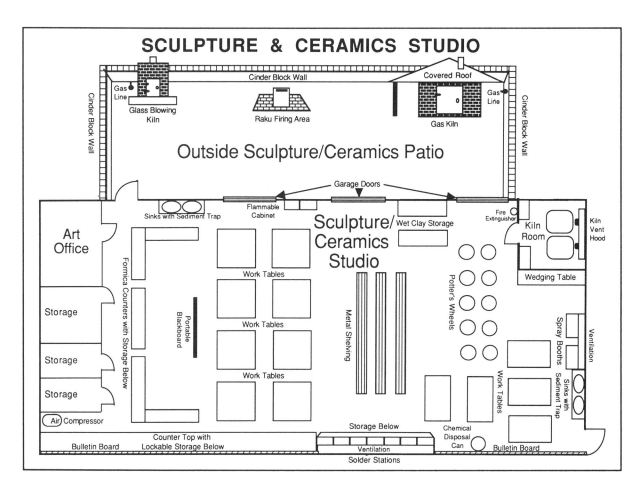

SCULPTURE & CERAMICS STUDIO

Cinder Block Wall

Covered Roof

Gas Line

Glass Blowing Kiln

Raku Firing Area

Gas Kiln

Gas Line

Cinder Block Wall

Cinder Block Wall

Outside Sculpture/Ceramics Patio

Garage Doors

Sinks with Sediment Trap

Flammable Cabinet

Sculpture/ Ceramics Studio

Wet Clay Storage

Fire Extinguisher

Kiln Room

Kiln Vent Hood

Art Office

Formica Counters with Storage Below

Work Tables

Portable Blackboard

Work Tables

Metal Shelving

Potter's Wheels

Wedging Table

Storage

Storage

Storage

Air Compressor

Work Tables

Spray Booths

Ventilation

Sinks with Sediment Trap

Work Tables

Storage Below

Chemical Disposal Can

Counter Top with Lockable Storage Below

Bulletin Board

Ventilation

Bulletin Board

Solder Stations

GENERAL SPECIFICATIONS

Overview

The teaching of art requires large spaces. Rooms must have secured in-room storage, adequately large sinks, and good lighting. The capability for showing slides both during the day and in the evening must be planned for as well as controlling the sound levels when showing films. General and local ventilation systems are needed to remove fumes and to make the air safe for both students and teachers. The rooms must be accessible to persons with physical impairments and a resource library center is needed within art rooms at all three levels. If plans call for two or more studios in a school, clustering them is not only logical but also facilitates team teaching.

Right and far right: Sarah W. Starkweather Elementary School, West Chester Area School District, West Chester, PA.

Space

Because student art projects may be one to two feet high and/or wide, art rooms need to be larger than general classrooms. NAEA recommends 55 square feet per student not including storage, kiln rooms, and teacher's offices and a maximum pupil/teacher ratio of 28:1. This leads to an art room covering 1,540 square feet (number of students x recommended square footage of 55 per student) excluding auxiliary space. NAEA recommends 400 square feet for the storage room, 45 square feet for the kiln room, and 120 square feet for the teacher's office. Additional space needs for a studio(s) appear later in this document.

Top: Sliding board unit. George Smith Middle School, Solanco School District, Quarryville, PA.
Middle: Teacher desk with demonstration mirror. George Smith Middle School, Solanco School District, Quarryville, PA.
Bottom: Painting area with storage units. Ralph M. Captain School, Clayton, MO.

Location

The art room should be on the first or ground floor, adjacent to a service entrance, the auditorium, and parking areas. An entrance door larger than the usual classroom door will allow for installation of bulky art equipment, such as kilns, drying racks, and printing presses. Planners who cluster the art room with the music room, theater/drama room, and dance studio facilitate cooperative activities among the other arts.

Patio

A patio with sliding glass door can provide auxiliary space for display, a natural light source, and a space for individual and group work.

Lighting

Color/visual perception is an essential component of art instruction. Thus, it is important to provide as much natural light as possible. General lighting should be planned so that shadows are reduced to a minimum in all parts of the room and all students have excellent visibility for their work. Every attempt should be made to simulate natural light as closely as possible.

Walls/Floors

Two criteria should determine the color selected for the art room walls: illumination and aesthetic appeal. Intense colors should be avoided throughout the art room(s) with neutral colors especially important in exhibition areas. Large sections of walls not covered by cabinets can be covered with tack board for additional display surfaces. A chalkboard six to twelve feet in length is sufficient for an art room.

The floors should be subdued colors of easy-to-maintain materials and have a non-slip surface, even when wet. A separate wet area with a sink is desirable for clay work. If a patio is provided, the wet area should be located in proximity to it.

Acoustics

The room should be acoustically treated to minimize the interferences of one group with another as well as with nearby classrooms.

Above top: Island sinks. George Smith Middle School, Solanco School District, Quarryville, PA.
Above middle: Counter (triple) sink. D.H. Conley High School, Pitt County Schools, Greenville, NC.
Bottom: Island sinks. Hattiesburg High School, Hattiesburg, MS.
Above right: Double Peninsula sink, Putnam City High School, Oklahoma City, OK.

Sinks

Art room sinks should be
1) Acid resistant.
2) Equipped with hot and cold running water.
3) Fitted with mixing faucets.
4) Made of stainless steel or other materials that do not chip, crack, or break.
5) Surrounded with a waterproof work surface.

Acid resistant, heavy duty drains with clay or plaster traps will prevent clogging. Sinks should be large enough (19" x 24" x 14") to accommodate several students concurrently at the sinks. Island or peninsula sinks are desirable in some situations because they are accessible from three sides. However, unless carefully situated, they might limit flexibility of the art room. NAEA recommends one sink per 10 students.

Security

Secure the special art storage areas, work stations, and supply areas against vandalism and theft of art materials and student works. It is also necessary to plan for the secure storage of potentially hazardous equipment and supplies.

Barrier-Free Design

The art room should be accessible to all students, including those with physical disabilities. For example, art areas should be wheelchair accessible including beneath work-top surfaces. (See Resource section.)

Examples of hooded kiln exhaust systems.
Top: Sarah Starkweather Elementary School,
West Chester School District, West Chester, PA.
Bottom: Ralph M. Captain School, Clayton, MO.
Opposite: Caraway Intermediate School,
Aldine ISD, Aldine, TX.

Safety

The importance of providing a safe environment cannot be over-emphasized. Facility planners should, from the earliest conception of new or remodeled space, consult with local, state, and federal agencies to become knowledgeable of all applicable safety requirements. The art room is the scene of many simultaneous activities and the need for safety precautions are special to each area. Thus, planners must establish proper precautions for each condition, such as good lighting, adequate ventilation, and floor drainage.

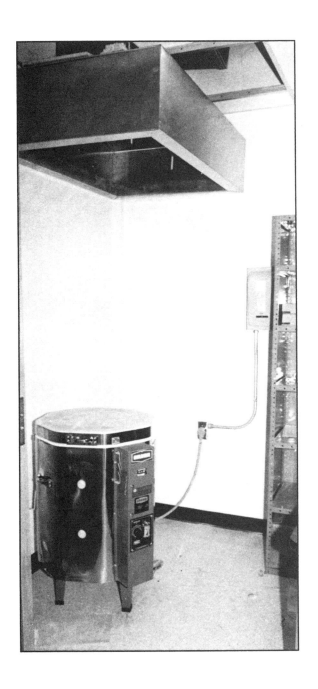

Art rooms must be ventilated. The ventilating system should be sufficient to handle fumes, odors, and dust generated by art activities. Both general and local exhaust systems are needed.

Special areas such as the kiln room, jewelry bench, pug mill, burnout kilns, printmaking, and photography require additional specific ventilation, most likely beyond existing codes.

Electric outlets should be plentiful throughout the art rooms to avoid the use of extension cords.

Equipment manufacturer's specific electric requirements for kilns and burn-out station should be known and properly provided. Separate circuits are required for potter's wheels.

AV, Computers, and Multimedia

Art room facilities must accommodate extensive use of audiovisual equipment needed for films, slides, computers, VCR's, and the like. Thus rooms should be equipped with a screen and black-out blinds and other room darkening features. It is also important to provide a dust-free environment for computers and multimedia hardware.

SPECIALIZED ART ROOMS

Studios—specialized rooms for work in particular media—are recommended according to the following ratio based on school population:

1) schools with 500 students or less—
   1 general art room
2) schools with 501-999 students—
   1 "two-dimensional art" room and
   1 "three-dimensional art" room
3) schools with 1,000 or more students—
   3 specialized studios (2 "two dimensional" and 1 "three-dimensional media").

Schools with more than 1,000 students should have one or more specialized art rooms to permit types of work not possible in a general

art room. Again, depending upon the student body size, the planners may select studios for drawing, painting, photography (including darkroom), ceramics, sculpture, printmaking, jewelry, textiles, computers, or multimedia.

Photography

Photography should be provided as part of the art program. Area requirements are a minimum of 340 square feet:

1) 100 square feet for film developing and chemical mixing
2) 180 square feet for dark room printing
3) 60 square feet for finishing.

Larger schools need an additional 80 square feet for an auxiliary dark room to handle color sheet film work. Safety factors are significantly elevated with the use of color film. Black and white set-ups are not adequate for color use.

Opposite: Bank of electric potter's wheels and standing pottery kickwheel in three-dimensional specialized art room.
Above: View of pug mill, wedging board, and band saw in three-dimensional specialized art room. Both photographs are from Putnam City High School, Oklahoma City, OK.

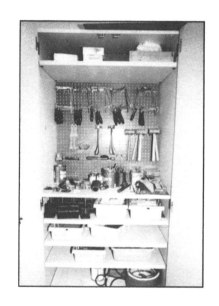

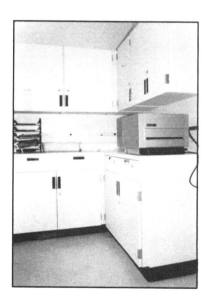

Top left: Computer lab. Rose HS, Greenville, NC.
Top right: Teacher art office. Spring High School, Aldine ISD, Aldine, TX.
Middle left: Art storeroom with metal shelving. Caraway Intermediate School, Aldine ISD, Aldine, TX.
Middle right: Lockable jewelry storage cabinet. Spring High School, Aldine, TX.
Left: Photography work area with lockable storage and print dryer. Spring High School, Aldine, TX.

Note that the photography room meets the stringent ventilation standards for such a facility and that all drain piping in the dark room is acid resistant.

Ceramics

Ceramics requires special equipment and storage facilities. Space should accommodate clay bins that are rust-proof, leak-proof, air tight, and portable. Facilities should also accommodate such special equipment as potter's wheels and a damp box (cabinet) for storing work in progress. Appropriate ventilation must be provided for any clay and glaze mixing.

Kiln Room

The electric kiln needs 45 square feet. Also needed is a special wiring circuit to meet kiln manufacturer's requirements and state and local codes. The kiln room must be ventilated to the outside to remove fumes as well as heat build-up. Metal storage cabinets for storing kiln shelves, shelf supports, stilts, and kiln wash should also be provided.

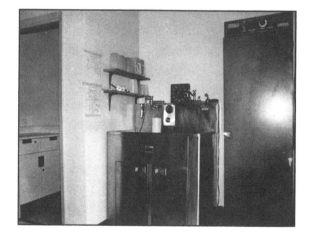

Top: Computer Stations. Rose High School, Greenville,NC.
Middle: Computer Room. Spring High School, Aldine ISD, Aldine, TX.
Bottom: Computer Lab. Putnam High School, Oklahoma City Schools, Oklahoma City, OK.

Top: Computer animation stations. Rose High School, Greenville, NC.
Middle: Photography darkroom. Note rotating print washer in foreground. Spring HS, Aldine ISD, Aldine, TX.
Bottom: Photography sink and negative dryer. Note loading room to left. Spring HS, Aldine ISD, Aldine, TX.

Teacher's Office and Work Station

The teacher's office and work space of 120 square feet is needed to house several filing cabinets, bookshelves, a teacher's desk, and a large drafting table. A glass-enclosed office is preferable.

Printmaking

While basic printmaking activities can be carried out on tables, special equipment is required for some procedures. Facilities should accommodate such equipment as printing press(es) and drying racks. Care must be taken to provide adequate ventilation for the use of inks and solvents and for drying prints (see Safety section). Eye wash fountains and emergency showers may be required if acids are used in any processess.

Storage Areas

The most crucial area in an art room is the storage space. There are five main types of storage:
1) Reserve
2) Work in Progress
3) Active
4) Portfolio
5) Potentially Hazardous Materials and Equipment

Above left: Teacher planning office. Winter Haven High School, Winter Haven, FL.
Above right: Computer stations, Winter Haven High School, Winter Haven, FL.

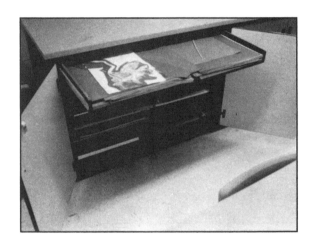

Top left: Student storage drawers. Hattiesburg High School, Hattiesburg, MS.
Above: Flat storage for student work-in-progress; *Top right:* Student storage lockers under work table. D.H. Conley High School, Pitt County Schools, Greenville, NC.
Below left: Computer lab storage drawers. Rose High School, Greenville, NC.
Opposite page, Top left: Portable student tote/storage trays. George C. Smith Middle School, Solanco School District, Quarryville, PA.
Top right: Sliding chalkboard unit with art resource library. D.H. Conley High School, Pitt County Schools, Greenville, NC.
Middle left: Shelving and display case. Starkweather Elementary School, West Chester Area School District, West Chester, PA.
Middle right: Table top art work drying rack. George C. Smith Middle School, Quarryville, PA.
Bottom left: Clay storage unit. D.H. Conley High School, Pitt County Schools, Greenville, NC.
Bottom right: Student lockers with storage above in 3-D studio. Putnam City High School, Oklahoma City, OK.

Generally 400 square feet of storage is necessary. This space should be divided as educational requirements dictate among storage for student works in progress, art supplies, and equipment. Shelving located in storage areas should accommodate the diversity of art instruction needs; it should handle, for example, the 22" x 24" dimensions of a standard size poster and the standard size matte board of 36" x 40". Appropriate lockable and vented storage must also be provided for flammable and combustible materials.

General Display Area

A display area—wall cabinets, bulletin boards, or the like—central to the general flow of school traffic should be provided. A porous material that accommodates hanging devices like pins, staples, and tracks is needed along with ceiling hooks for hanging three-dimensional artwork.

30

Student art galleries. *Opposite top:* Note adjustable ceiling spotlights, Putnam City High School, Oklahoma City, OK. *Opposite bottom:* Art room entry gallery, Winter Haven High School, Winter Haven, FL.

These areas should be well lighted and equipped with multiple lighting plug-in track with movable spotlights. A portable display system is desirable. If the display area is not secure, key locks should be installed on display doors.

Resource Library

There should be an area dedicated to films, slide collections and resources for instructional units in the art program. Major collections of books, prints, software, tapes, cassettes, disks, catalogs, and media, should be housed in the main school library and art students should be scheduled to conduct research and art study on a regular basis. Similarly, art career collections should be housed in the career center/counselor's office and students scheduled on a regular basis to research career opportunities.

Technology

The use of computers, laser printers, scanners, camcorders, and other high tech video equipment is rapidly being employed in art education programs. Examples include use of imagery research and instruction with laser disks, desktop and graphic design, as well as computer generated art work. Two applications are currently being used:

1) in the art room as a learning/research station (i.e., 2-5 computers, printers, etc.).
2) in a dedicated lab or media center, in which students are scheduled by class or via independent study (i.e. 25-30 computer stations, printers, modems, laser disks, scanners, camcorders, etc.).

Conclusion

This guide is intended to serve as a general frame of reference for school art facilities planning. Each state has different requirements i.e., type of lighting, mechanical, electrical, plumbing and other architectural specifications that depend on individual locations, local and state codes, and the like. Additionally, schools vary in their art curriculum requirements, thus will vary in the needed art facility designs. In choosing equipment and/or fixtures, manufacturers' guidelines can also provide important information. Perhaps the most important aspect of planning an artroom is simply that — planning first and carefully can lead to exciting art experiences for the most number of students attending school for the next several generations. Because it is not unusual for schools to be operational for some 40 to 50 or more years, it is even more imperative that school decision-makers and art educators make substantive investments in careful planning of the school art facility.

Resources

There are many sources that provide specific technical assistance to the art facility planner. Many provide guidelines while others might provide legislative requirements or simply contacts for further information. Because products and equipment change from year to year it is not unreasonable that codes and other requirements change also. The following list of resources are some of the obvious sources to provide assistance. This listing is by no means exhaustive; we do however hope it provides a comprehensive starting point.

STATE DEPARTMENTS OF EDUCATION: In addition to the expertise of local school and district art educators and administrators, another resource is the state department of education. Many state departments of education have visual arts education offices, offices for disabled students, school facilities offices, general administrative and financial offices that can be a resource for guidelines, procedures, codes, or other state requirements. Addresses for state departments of education and the above offices may be secured from your local school district.

MANUFACTURERS: Guidelines for specifications on fixtures and equipment are important information in planning the art facility. For a listing of NAEA vendors,

exhibitors, and advertisers, contact the NAEA office at 1916 Association Dr., Reston, VA 20191-1590. Other sources of manufacturers are the **National Art Materials Trade Association,** 178 Lakeview Ave., Clifton, NJ 07011; **National School Supply & Equipment Association,** 8300 Colesville Road, Suite 250, Silver Spring, MD 20910; and the editor of *Arts and Crafts Retailer*, 6151 Powers Ferry Road, NW, Atlanta, GA 30339-2941.

SUPPLY COMPANIES: Suppliers' catalogs provide general information about equipment and material, especially about safety and health. Several include: **Direct Safety Company,** 7815 South 46th St., Phoenix, AZ; **Henry's Safety Supply Co.,** 14252 West 44th Ave., Golden, CO 80403; **Lab Safety Supply,** P.O. Box 1366, Janesville, WI 53547.

ORGANIZATIONS: Many organizations provide excellent educational materials that apply to supplies, equipment, and materials used in the art room. Some important organizations are: **The Art and Craft Materials Institute,** 100 Boylston St., Suite 1050, Boston, MA 02116; **American National Standards Institute,** 655 15th St., N.W., Suite 300, Washington, DC 20005; **Association of School Business Officials,** 11401 North Shore Dr., Reston, VA 22090-4232; **Barrier Free Environments, Inc.,** P.O. Box 30634, Raleigh, NC 27622; **Council of Educational Facility Planners, International,** 29 West Woodruff Ave., Columbus, OH 43210; **Center for Safety in the Arts,** 5 Beekman St., Suite 1030, New York, NY 10038; **Council for Exceptional Children,** 1920 Association Dr., Reston VA 20191; **Hazards in the Arts,** 5340 N. Magnolia, Chicago, IL 60640; **National Association of Photographic Manufacturers, Inc.,** 550 Mamaroneck Ave., Harrison, NY 10528-1612; **National Safety Council,** 444 North Michigan Ave., Chicago, IL 60611.

FEDERAL AGENCIES: **Architectural and Transportation Barriers Compliance Board,** 1111 18th St., N.W., Suite 501, Washington, DC 20036; **Consumer Product Safety Commission,** 1111 18th St., N.W., Washington, DC 20036; **Environmental Protection Agency,** 401 M St., S.W., Washington, DC 20460; **National Institute for Occupational Safety and Health,** 4676 Columbia Parkway, Cincinnati, OH 45226; **Occupational Safety and Health Administration,** Department of Labor, 200 Constitution Ave., N.W., Washington, DC 20210; For ADA implementation issues at the local or state level, please call the **National Institute on Disabilities, Rehabilitation, and Research,** 1-800-949-4232.

NAEA SCHOOL ART FACILITIES AWARD

The National Art Education Association *School Art Facilities Program Award* is one of the most prestigious awards that an elementary, middle, junior, or senior high school art program can receive. This NAEA award recognizes exemplary art facilities in individual schools and entire school systems which meet the standards set forth in the *Design Standards for School Art Facilities* publication.

This publication provides a general planning reference for facilities. It sets forth standards for elementary, middle, junior, or senior high school art rooms and is intended to be used as an integral part of the nomination process. It should be referred to as ratings are determined for the checklist. The standards are divided into categories — *Planning an Art Room*, *General Specifications*, and *Specialized Art Rooms*. These standards address space, location, lighting, walls and floors, acoustics, sinks, security, accessibility, safety, and technology.

Nomination/Eligibility Application

Applications may be made any time during the school year (July 1 to June 30). Elementary, middle, junior, or senior high schools can be nominated by completing the *Nomination Form* and *Checklist* and sending it to the Awards Coordinator, National Art Education Association, 1916 Association Drive, Reston, Virginia 20191-1590.

Membership Fees

A local education agency fee is required for each application. This fee is equivalent to the regular active NAEA member fee and indicates that the art educator at the facility is a member in good standing of the Association. The local education agency fee is waived if the art facility nominator is a current Active member or the school is a current Institutional member of NAEA. Local education agency fees may be paid by an individual, school, district, or community group/agency. A listing of the state schedule for membership dues is included on the nomination form.

NAEA *Design Standards for School Art Facilities*

NOMINATION FORM AND CHECKLIST

This checklist is designed for schools wishing to nominate their art facilities for recognition as exemplary by the National Art Education Association. The checklist is to be completed in conjunction with the *Design Standards for School Art Facilities* publication. Applicants should enter **M** if their facilitity **meets or exceeds** the standards; **minus [-]** if it **does not** meet the standards. The checklist must be signed by the individual completing the nomination and co-signed by the appropriate school administrator. The Assurance must be signed and dated by the Superintendent.

-Please Print or Type-

Date _____ School _____

School Address _____
                            Street/PO Box   City   State   Zip + 4

School Phone _____ School Art Teacher _____

Grade Level _____ School Principal _____

We hereby testify that _____ school meets or exceeds the standards set forth by the NAEA *Design Standards for School Art Facilities*.

_____   _____
         Nominating Teacher's Signature   Administrator's Signature

ASSURANCE: I do hereby certify that all information on this application is true and correct to the best of my knowledge and belief. I further certify that the facilities addressed in this application meet or exceed the standards set forth in the *Design Standards for School Arts Facilities* publication.

Date _____ Superintendent's Signature _____

──── NAEA STANDARDS AWARD FEES ────

NAEA ID# _____ Expiration Date _____
        *Local Education Agency Fee (see Dues Schedule below) $ _____

No fee required if the art faculty is a current NAEA member or the school is an Institutional member.

You will receive a paper certificate free of charge, for an additional $25 you may order a 6' x 9' walnut plaque which features a ceramic insert with the NAEA seal and a brass plate engraved with your school name.

                                      Walnut Plaque (optional) $ _____
                                      Total Amount Enclosed $ _____

Send full payment to: Awards Coordinator, NAEA, 1916 Association Dr., Reston, VA 20191-1590

EFFECTIVE JULY 1, 2001 to JUNE 30, 2004

These fees include state and national dues: CT, RI $80; AL AZ, KS, MI, NC $75; PA $74; CO, DC, DE, IA, VA, WV, WY $70; AR, GA, HI, IN, LA, MA, MO, MT, NE, NM, NV, OK, OR, SC, TN, WA, WI, Overseas Art Education $65; SD $60.

These fees include national dues only: CA, FL, ID, IL, KY, ME, MN, MS, NH, NJ, NY, ND, OH, TX, US Possessions, UT, VT, Canadian/Foreign $50.

*A **Local Education Agency Fee** is required. This fee is equivalent to the regular active NAEA member fee. This enables the individual or institution sponsoring the Standards Award to be a member in good standing in the NAEA.

PLANNING THE ART ROOM (See pages 1-13)

_____ Thoughtful planning and consideration was given to the facility and the amount of money made available for it.

_____ The art room is specialized and flexible to meet the needs of a diversified program.

_____ The art teacher was involved in budget and design decisions.

_____ The facility is flexible enough to accommodate student discussions, group work, slide viewing, reproductions,and computers.

_____ Adequate space (square footage), including storage, display, and a range of equipment are provided.

_____ Special provisions were made for equipment mobility, flexibility, and accessibility and for making a variety of materials available quickly and systematically.

_____ The number of art rooms per school meets the NAEA student/teacher ratio.

_____ General lighting is planned so that shadows are reduced to a minimum.

_____ Sinks are accessible from several sides and are appropriate height for grade levels and wheel chairs.

_____ Sinks are equipped with hot and cold water with sediment traps.

_____ The room layout allows for ease of traffic flow and safety.

GENERAL SPECIFICATIONS (See pages 14-21)

_____ The capability exists for showing slides, films or videos during the day and evening.

_____ An entrance door larger than usual allows for installation of bulky art equipment.

_____ The art room is accoustically treated to minimize interferences.

_____ Acid resistant, heavy duty drains with clay or plaster traps are provided.

_____ Adequate securable space is provided for storing hazardous equipment and supplies.

_____ The art room is accessible to all students, including those with physical disabilities.

_____ Special areas (kiln, pug mill, etc.) are equipped with adequate ventilation.

_____ Electrical outlets are plentiful and conveniently located throughout the art room.

_____ The art room facilitates extensive use of audio/visual equipment, VCR's, computers, etc.

SPECIALIZED ART ROOMS (See pages 22-31)

_____ Schools with 1,000 enrollment provide one or more specialized art rooms.

_____ Specialized art rooms are equipped to provide in-depth experiences.

_____ Adequate teacher office and work stations that meet NAEA standards are provided.

_____ Display areas are central to the general flow of traffic.

_____ An area is dedicated to films, slide collections, and other instructional materials.